PUFFIN BOOKS

Published by the Penguin Group
27 Wrights Lane, London W8 5TZ, England
Viking Penguin, a division of Penguin Books USA Inc, 375 Hudson Street, New York, New York 10014, USA
Penguin Books Australia Ltd, Ringwood, Victoria, Australia
Penguin Books Canada Ltd, 10 Alcorn Avenue, Toronto, Ontario, Canada M4V 3B2
Penguin Books (NZ) Ltd, 182-190 Wairau Road, Auckland 10, New Zealand
Penguin Books SA, Amethyst Street, Theta Ext 1, Johannesburg, South Africa

Penguin Books Ltd, Registered Offices: Harmondsworth, Middlesex, England

First published by Puffin Books 1995

This collection © Susan Cock and Marilyn Wood, 1995
All rights reserved
The moral right of the compilers has been asserted

ISBN 0 140 37987 8

Musical arrangement : 'Never kick a toadstool', 'Alphabet Soup' and 'God Bless Africa' © Susan Cock, 1995;
'Treintjie Speel' and 'Natuursang' © Salóme Hendrikse
Illustrations © Ulla Blake, 1995

Cover and text design and illustrations by Ulla Blake
Music typeset by Mariaan van Kaam; other typesetting by Marilyn Wood

Printed by National Book Printers, Drukkery Street, Goodwood, Western Cape
Except in the United States of America, this book is sold subject to the condition that it shall not, by way of trade or otherwise, be lent, resold, hired out, or otherwise circulated without the publisher's prior consent in any form of binding or cover other than that in which it is published and without a similar condition including this condition being imposed on the subsequent purchaser.

CONTENTS

Greeting Songs

Siyanibulisa	isiZulu	5
Say Hello	English	6
Hello Lungile	seSotho	7

Sleeping and Waking Songs

Slaap kindjie, slaap	Afrikaans	8
Thula Thu'	isiZulu	9
Just let me wake up	English	10
Vukani madoda	isiZulu	11

Food Songs

Ge re sila	seTswana	13
O jele tamati	seSotho	14
Peanut Butter Rondo	English	15
Tamati sososo	isiZulu	16
Silang mabele	sePedi	17

Travel Songs

Treintjie Speel	Afrikaans	18
Shosholoza	isiZulu	22
Ke ne ke nkile	seSotho	25
EMonti	isiZulu	26

Nature and Weather Songs

Pula ya na	seTswana	27
Natuursang	Afrikaans	28
Never kick a toadstool	English	31

Animal and Bird Songs

Nganginehhashi	isiZulu	32
Tweba dili tharo	seTswana	33
Wen' osematholeni	isiZulu	34
Alphabet Soup	English	35
Impuku nekati	isiXhosa	46
Demazana	isiZulu	47

Love, Wedding and Dance Songs

Maatjie klein	Afrikaans	48
Punchinello	English	49
Fiela	seSotho	50
Baba Mnumzane	isiZulu	51
Ra šila mielie	sePedi	53
If the world	English	54

Religious Songs

Uthando lwakhe	isiZulu	55
Tshollela	seSotho	56
Thuma mina	isiZulu	58
God Bless Africa	English	59
Ukuthula	isiZulu	60

Pronunciation guide 62

Rhymes

Handjies klap, voetjies stap	Afrikaans	6
Mapimpane	seSotho	8
Nonyane tse tlhano	seTswana	10
My mother, your mother	English	13
Tararara boemdery	Afrikaans	14
Ngineminwe emihlanu	isiZulu	15
Mankokosane	seSotho	17
Izinyoni ezinhlanu	isiZulu	19
Duimelot	Afrikaans	20
Sawubona we katshana	isiZulu	21
Tselane	seSotho	23
Handjies klap, koekies bak	Afrikaans	24
Three little monkeys	English	26
Luphi ulwandle?	isiZulu	29
Duimpie	Afrikaans	30
One, two, three, four, five	English	33
Dinonyana tse hlano	seSotho	34
Kwesukesukel' uGege	isiZulu	43
Ngubani lo?	isiZulu	45
Trippe trappe trone	Afrikaans	46
Molo we katshana	isiXhosa	47
Mina ngiyisicathulo	isiZulu	48
Ke mmutlanyana	seSotho	52
Vuka mfana	isiZulu	54
I see the moon	English	55

INTRODUCTION

'Music is the universal language of mankind'
(Henry Wadsworth Longfellow)

Through music we can bridge the gap of language, cultures and age. We can express joy, sorrow, pleasure. And singing is a medium that is open to everybody. Through singing, we can meet, we learn other languages, other ideas, other rhythms of life. We can enjoy each other's company as in no other medium. In *Spot on Song Book* we aim to provide, through song and rhyme, a little of that joy and pleasure which is part of the musical culture and tradition in South Africa.

Spot on Song Book is aimed primarily at junior school second language learners. However, adult second language learners can also enjoy the excitement of learning about the languages and cultures of South Africa.

None of these songs or rhymes pretends to be the 'official' traditional version. We have taken songs as people sing them: in some cases they have stayed the same for many years, but in others the songs have been adapted as they have travelled into the cities. As is the nature of oral tradition, there will always be other ways to sing them.

Songs have been carefully chosen so that the level of the language and the music complement each other. The degree of difficulty of each song is indicated by a symbol as follows:

easy song

medium difficulty

more complex

To help teachers and others unfamiliar with the languages, all the songs and rhymes have been recorded on cassette so that the pronunciation can be heard. Pronunciation guidelines are also given on pages 62 - 64.

As well as the more detailed list of acknowledgements which follows, our thanks are also due to Ulla Blake, whose enthusiastic contribution went well beyond the layout and art work.

Acknowledgements

The compilers and publisher would like to thank the following people and organizations for their contributions to this book:

Teachers at Ukukhanya Kwe Zwe, Malborough; Anne Fairfax, teachers and children at the Orange Grove Early Learning Centre; Teachers and children at the D D Lewayo pre-school, Orlando; Gail Dymond and children at the Vuleka School, Auckland Park; Lizzie Hlapolasa and Maria Masilela from Monahan Farm; Miriam Schiff and the Orff Society; Renette Bouwer for the Afrikaans rhymes; Salóme Hendrikse for some of the Afrikaans songs; Estelle Rassmann; Mpho Hlabele, Itumileng Masako, Joyce Moholoagae, Florence Zungu, Phafuli Lehlohonolo, Joyce Mmusi, for help with the seSotho, sePedi and seTswana translation; Bonelela Mtambo and Thandiwe Nxumalo for help with the isiZulu and isiXhosa translation; Jeanne Snyman for help with the Afrikaans translation and pronunciation advice.

SIYANIBULISA
isiZulu

Siyanibulisa
Siyanibulisa
Bambani isandla
Siyanibulisa
Siyanibulisa
Bambani isandla

Bhekani izandla zethu
(Repeat three times)
zimhlophe qwa!
Tra la la la la la la
Bambani isandla.

We are greeting you
We are greeting you
Shake hands
We are greeting you
We are greeting you
Shake hands
Look at our hands
They are very clean
Tra la la la la la la
Shake hands.

SAY HELLO

English

Afrikaans

Handjies klap
Voetjies stap
Ogies kyk
Neusies snuit
Mondjies fluit
Kennebak
Gorrelgat
Doedelsak.

Little hands clap
Little feet stamp
Little eyes look
Little noses sniff
Little lips whistle
Chin-a-gin
Gurgle-bin
Tummykin.

Let us clap and say hello
(Repeat four times)
Let us stamp and say hello
(Repeat four times)
Let us shake and say hello
(Repeat four times)
Let us jump and say hello.
(Repeat four times)

HELLO LUNGILE

seSotho

Hello *Lungile*, hello *Lungile*,
hello *Lungile*, my girl
(Repeat)

Rona re palama tjhutjhu
Rona re palama tjhutjhu
Rona re palama tjhutjhu, my girl.
(Repeat)

Hello Lungile, hello Lungile,
hello Lungile, my girl

We are riding on the train
We are riding on the train
We are riding on the train,
my girl.

Substitute different girls' names in place of Lungile. For example:

Hello Winnie, hello Winnie,
Hello Winnie, my girl...

SLAAP KINDJIE SLAAP
Afrikaans

Slaap kind-jie, slaap. Daar bui-te loop 'n skaap. 'n Ska-pie met sy wit-te wol. Hy drink sy melk, sy ma-gie's vol. Slaap kind-jie, slaap.

seSotho

Mapimpane, Mapimpane
Ngwana wa ausi,
Tlo re ye sekolong
Mahlo ke hlapile
Hloho ke e kame
Tlapa la hao le kae?
Ruri ke le lebetse
Tlapa la hao le kae?
Ruri ke le lebetse.

Mapimpane, Mapimpane
Sister's child,
Come, let's go to school
I have washed my face
I have combed my hair
Where is your slate?
Indeed I have forgotten
Where is your slate?
Indeed I have forgotten.

Slaap kindjie, slaap
Daar buite loop 'n skaap
'n Skapie met sy witte wol
Hy drink sy melk
sy magie's vol
Slaap kindjie, slaap.

Sleep little one, sleep
Outside there's a sheep
A sheep with white wool
He drinks his milk
his stomach is full
Sleep little one, sleep.

THULA THU'

isiZulu

Thula thu' thula mntwana,
thula sana
Thul' umam' uzofika ekuseni
(Repeat)

Kukh' inkanyezi eholel' ubaba
Imkhanyisel' indlel' eziy' ekhaya.
(Repeat)

Hush, hush, hush child,
hush child
Hush, Mother is coming in the morning

There is a star guiding Father
Lighting up the way home for him.

English

JUST LET ME WAKE UP

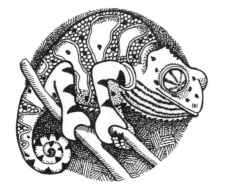

Just let me wake up in the early morn
(Repeat three times)
And I'll never sleep late anymore

Let me stand up and walk
around the world
(Repeat three times)
And I'll never sleep late anymore.

seTswana	Nonyane tse tlhano	Five birds
	godimo ga setlhare.	in a tree.
	E nngwe ya re,	One said,
	'Bona mole.'	'Look there.'
	E nngwe ya re,	One said,
	'Ke monna ka sethunya.'	'It is a man with a gun.'
	E nngwe ya re,	One said,
	'A re tshabeng.'	'Let's run away.'
	E nngwe ya re,	One said,
	'A re iphitleng.'	'Let's hide away.'
	E nngwe yare,	One said,
	'Ga re motshabe rona,	'We are not afraid,
	ga re motshabe rona.	we are not afraid.
	Re a fofa.	We are flying away.
	Re a fofa.'	We are flying away.'

VUKANI MADODA

isiZulu

Traditional Harmonies arr. Mzilikazi Khumalo

Vukani madoda
sekusile we mama
Vukani madoda
sekusile we mama
Lakhal' iqhude lathi,
'Kikilikigi'
Labhul' amaphiko lathi,
'Kikilikigi'
(Repeat)

Vukani madoda
sekusile madoda
Vukani madoda
kusile.

Wake up men
it is already dawn
Wake up men
it is already dawn
The cock crowed, saying
'Cock-a-doodle-doo'
It flapped its wings, saying
'Cock-a-doodle-doo'

Wake up men
it is already dawn men
Wake up men
it is dawn.

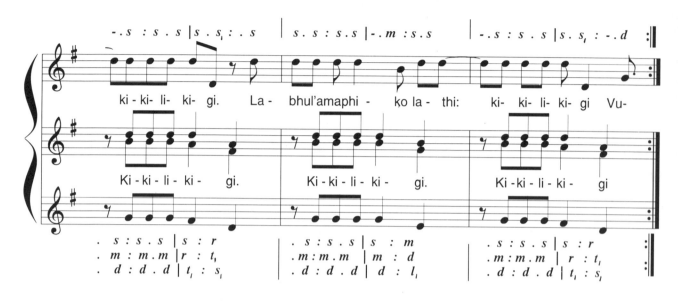

GE RE SILA

seTswana

Ge re sila lwa leng
Ge re sila lwa leng
Re re gwai, re re gwai,
re re gwai gwai gwai
Ge o tlile le tlatla
ya ga go e tletseng
o tla sila wa sila
wa be wa fetsa leng.

When we grind
on the grinding stone
We say: grrr
(*the sound of the stone*)
When you come
with your mielies
You will grind and grind
until you are finished.

My mother, your mother
live across the street.
Every night they have a fight
and this is what they say,
'Icky bicky, soda cracker
Icky bicky boo.
Icky bicky, soda cracker
Out goes you!'

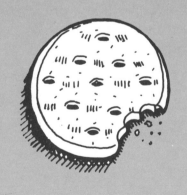

O JELE TAMATI

seSotho

O je- le ta- ma- ti e se- nang le- tswa -i. O je- le

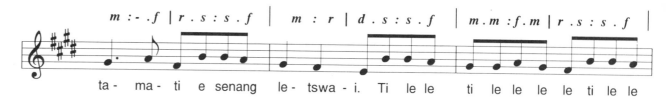
ta- ma- ti e senang le- tswa -i. Ti le le ti le le le le ti le le

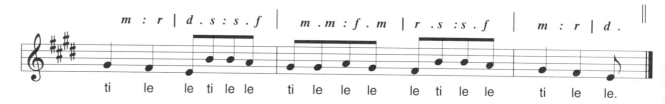
ti le le ti le le ti le le le le ti le le ti le le.

Afrikaans

Tararara boemdery
Oupa het 'n vark gery
Afgeval en seergekry
Opgeklim en weer gery
Tararara boemdery.

Tararara boemdery
Grandpa rode a pig
He fell off and hurt himself
He climbed back on
and rode again
Tararara boemdery.

O jele tamati e senang letswai
(Repeat)

Ti le le ti le le le le
ti le le ti le le
ti le le ti le le le le ti le le ti le le.

You ate a tomato without salt

Ti le le ti le le le le
ti le le ti le le
ti le le ti le le le le ti le le ti le le.

PEANUT BUTTER RONDO English

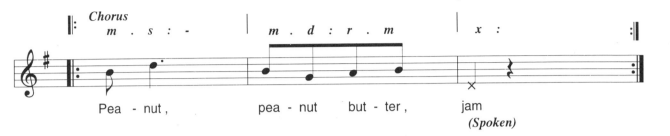

Peanut, peanut butter, jam
(Repeat)

First you dig 'em, dig 'em,
dig 'em, dig 'em, dig 'em.
Then you crush 'em, crush 'em,
crush 'em, crush 'em, crush 'em

Peanut, peanut butter, jam
(Repeat)

Then you pick 'em, pick 'em,
pick 'em, pick 'em, pick 'em
Then you squish 'em,
squash 'em, squish 'em,
squash 'em, squish 'em
Then you spread 'em,
spread 'em, spread 'em,
spread 'em, spread 'em

Peanut, peanut butter, jam
(Repeat)

Then you bite it, bite it, bite it,
bite it, bite it
Then you munch it, munch it,
munch it, munch it, munch it
Then you swallow, swallow,
swallow, swallow, swallow

Peanut, peanut butter, jam
(Said with tongue in cheek!)
(Repeat)

isiZulu

Ngineminwe emihlanu
engiyibiza ngamagama.
Uthuphazane lo -
isidludla sami lesi.
Ukhombisile lo -
umthethi wamacala.
Umdanyana lo -
yindoda enhle kakhulu.
Uthembisile lo -
umngane wendandathu.
Ucikicane lo -
ithemba lami leli.

I have five fingers
which I call by names.
This is the thumb -
my fat man, this one.
This is my pointing finger -
the talker in court.
The middle finger is this one -
the very handsome man.
The engagement finger is this one -
the friend of the wedding ring.
This is the little finger -
this one is my hope.

TAMATI SOSOSO

isiZulu

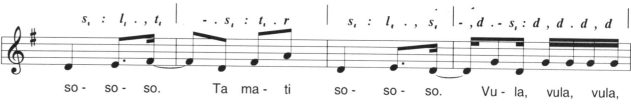
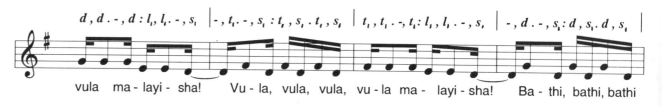

Tamati sososo
(Repeat four times)

Vula, vula, vula,
vula malayisha!
(Repeat)

Bathi, bathi,
bathi vula malayisha!
(Repeat)

Tomato sauce

Open, open, open,
open 'loader'!

They say, they say,
they say open 'loader'!

SILANG MABELE

sePedi

Silang mabele
Gamang dikgomo
Tsatsi le a phirima
Bana ba swere ke tlala
Ba swere ke ramatheka
Monna yo mosesane.

Grind the corn
Milk the cows
The sun is setting
The children are hungry
They have backache
This man is thin.

seSotho

Mankokosane
Pula e ya na
Re tla hola neng?

Mankokosane
It is raining
When will we grow?

TREINTJIE SPEEL

Afrikaans

Music: Salóme Hendrikse   Lyrics: Twinkle Hanekom

Pof, pof, pof, pof dwarsdeur die stof
Pietjie is die enjin, ons is die trein
Pof pof

Sakke pakke pof pof
Sakke pakke pof pof
Hier's die stasie
Stop! Stop!

Puff, puff, puff, puff
right through the dust
Pietjie is the engine, we are the train
Puff puff

Chugg chugg puff puff
Chugg chugg puff puff
Here is the station
Stop! Stop!

isiZulu

Izinyoni ezinhlanu
zazihlezi emthini.
Enye yathi,
'Kuyini lokhuya?'
Enye yathi,
'Indoda nesibhamu.'
Enye yathi, 'Masibalekene.'
Enye yathi, 'Masicashene.'
Enye yathi,
'Asimesabi thina,
asimesabi thina.'
Saqhuma isibhamu.
Zandiza ezine
yasala eyodwa.
Yasala seyifile.

Five birds
were sitting in a tree.
One said,
'What is that over there?'
One said,
'A man with a gun.'
One said, 'Let's run away.'
One said, 'Let's hide.'
One said,
'We are not afraid of him,
we are not afraid of him.'
The gun went bam!
Four flew away
and one remained.
It died.

Afrikaans

Duimelot het 'n os gekoop
Lekkepot het hom laat loop
Langeraat het hom afgeslag
Fielefooi het die wors gestop
en die klein man eet alles op!

Thumbelocks bought an ox
Lickapot fed it a lot
Long Tom slaughtered it well
Ringading stuffed the sausage
and the littlest one ate it all.

isiZulu

Sawubona we katshana
Uyaphi we katshana?
Ngiya edolobheni
Uyokuthenga yini?
Ngiyothenga isigqoko
Isigqoko?
Isigqoko?
Angizange ngilibone
ikati lithwele isigqoko!

Hello little cat
Where are you going, little cat?
I am going to town
To go and buy what?
I am going to go and buy a hat
A hat?
A hat?
I have never seen
a cat wearing a hat!

SHOSHOLOZA

isiZulu

Shosholoza x2
Uyeye
Kulezo ntaba
s'timela siphuma eSouth Africa
(Repeat)

Wen' uyabaleka
Uyeye
Kulezo ntaba
s'timela siphuma eSouth Africa.
(Repeat)

Shosholoza
Oh yea
From those mountains
the train comes from South Africa

You are running away
Oh yea
From those mountains
the train comes from South Africa.

seSotho

Tselane, ngwana ke
Tselane, ngwana ke
Nka nka bohobe o je
Tselane, ngwana ke.

Tselane, my child
Tselane, my child
Take the bread and eat
Tselane, my child.

Afrikaans

Handjies klap
Koekies bak
Gaan na die mark
Koop 'n stukkie vark
Koop 'n stukkie long
vir die siekie jong
Koop 'n stukkie lint
vir die sieke kind
Hier kom die krappie aangekruip
en onder die armpie ingeduik.

Clap your hands
Bake a cake
Run to the market
Fetch some pork
Buy a piece of lung
for the man so young
Buy a piece of ribbon
for the sickly child
Here comes the little crab
and crawls under your arm.

KE NE KE NKILE

seSotho

Ke ne ke nkile leeto
Ke ile ka per' e tshweu
ha ke bona perekisi e ntle
hara tshimo ya hao
Pere e tshweu

ke romile mang?
(Repeat three times)

Pere e tshweu
ke romile mang?

I took a journey
I went on a white horse
when I saw a nice peach
in your field
White horse,
whom did I send?
White horse,
whom did I send?

EMONTI

isiZulu

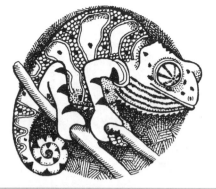

Three little monkeys
jumping on a bed
One fell off and
bumped his head
Mama called the doctor
and the doctor said,
'No more monkeys
jumping on the bed!'

Two little monkeys
jumping on a bed
One fell off and
bumped his head
Mama called the doctor
and the doctor said,
'No more monkeys
jumping on the bed!'

One little monkey
jumping on the bed
He fell off and
bumped his head
Mama called the doctor
and the doctor said,
'No more monkeys
jumping on the bed!'

EMonti
(Repeat six times)

NabaseKapa
bavelel' eMonti.
(Repeat)

East London
Even those in Cape Town
come from East London.

PULA YA NA

seTswana

Pula ya na, mogatsame
A me ha e ne, mogatsame?
Re tlo lema, mogatsame
Re tlo lema, mogatsame
Pula ya na, mogatsame
A me ha e ne, mogatsame?
Re tlo lema, mogatsame.

It rained, my spouse
Is it not raining, my spouse?
We will plough, my spouse
We will plough, my spouse
Is it not raining, my spouse?
We will plough, my spouse.

NATUURSANG

Afrikaans

Music: Salóme Hendrikse   Lyrics: Anon

Wat sê die wind as hy saggies suis?
Woemm, woemm, woemm!
Wat sê die see as die water bruis?
Boemm, boemm, boemm!
Wat sê die reen as dit spitter en spat?
Tippetetap tippetetap,
tippete, tippete, tippetap!
Wat sê die hael op ons dakke so plat?
Klippeteklap, klippeteklap,
klippete, klippeteklap!

What does the wind say
in its soft murmur?
Voomm, voomm, voomm!
What does the sea say
in the thunder of the waves?
Boomm, boomm, boomm!
What does the rain say
as it spitter-spatters?
Tip tap, tip tap, tip tap
tip-a-tap, tip-a-tap, tap
What does the hail say
on our roofs so flat?
Clippety clap, clippety clap,
clippety, clippety clap.

isiZulu

Luphi ulwandle?
LuseThekwini
Luphi ulwandle?
LuseThekwini
Lwenzani?
Lugubh' amagagasi
Lwenzani?
Lugubh' amagagasi.

Where is the sea?
It is in Durban
Where is the sea?
It is in Durban
What does the sea do?
The waves tumble about
What does the sea do?
The waves tumble about.

Afrikaans

Duimpie het in die put geval
Lekkepot het hom uitgehaal
Langeraat het hom huistoe gedra
Fielefooi het hom neergelê
en pinkie het vir ma gaan sê.

Thumbelocks fell in a well
Lickalot pulled him out
Long Tom carried him home
Ringaround lay him down
and Pinkypom ran to Mom.

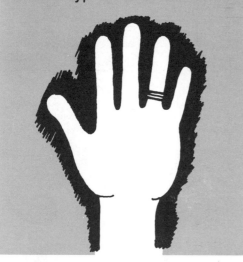

NEVER KICK A TOADSTOOL English

Music: Sue Cock Lyrics: Ashleigh Blackman

Never kick a toadstool - that is the rule!
For it might be the house of a tiny wee mouse.

NGANGINEHHASHI

isiZulu

Ehhe! Nganginehhashi elimhlophe
elalihamba lenze nje
(Repeat)

EMarabini - elalihamba lenze nje.
(Repeat)

Yes! I had a white horse
that pranced like this

At Marabini - which pranced like this.

TWEBA DILI THARO

seTswana

Tweba dili tharo
(Repeat)
tse di foufetseng
(Repeat)
Mosadi mogolo wa lekgo'
A di tabogisa ka thip' e kana.

Three mice
who were blind
A big white woman
chased them with a knife this big.

One, two, three, four, five
Once I caught a fish alive
Six, seven, eight, nine, ten
Then I let him go again
Why did you let him go?
Because he bit my finger so
Which finger did he bite?
This little finger on the right.

WEN' OSEMATHOLENI

isiZulu

Wen' o-se-ma-tho-le-ni i-ju-ba yi-jah'e-li-khu-lu.

Vu-ma mtsheke-tshe-ke! I-ya-khala le nyo-ni.

Wen' osematholeni
ijuba yijah' elikhulu
Vuma mtsheketsheke!
Iyakhala le nyoni.

You who tend the calves
The dove is very strong
Agree ant!
This bird is crying.

*Substitute these bird names
for 'ijuba' in subsequent verses:*

isikhova	owl
inkonjane	swallow
igwababa	crow
intinginono	secretary bird
inqe	vulture
ukhozi	black mountain eagle

This is a traditional song intended as a game to teach children the names of birds. Individuals would sing the song substituting different bird names until they were unable to do so. The next person would then have a turn.

seSotho	Dinonyana tse hlano	Five birds
	di ne di dutse sefateng.	were sitting in a tree.
	E nngwe ya re,	One said,
	'Ke eng hoo?'	'What is that?'
	E nngwe ya re,	One said,
	'Ke monna ka sethunya.'	'A man with a gun.'
	E nngwe ya re,	One said,
	'Ha re baleheng.'	'Let's run away.'
	E nngwe ya re,	One said,
	'Ha re ipateng.'	'Let's hide.'
	E nngwe ya re,	One said,
	'Ha re mo tshabe rona,	'We are not scared of him,
	ha re mo tshabe rona.'	we are not scared of him.'
	Thu ka sethunya.	The gun went off.
	Thu ka sethunya.	The gun went off.
	Thu ka sethunya.	The gun went off.
	Tse nne tsa fofa.	Four flew away.
	Ha sala e le nngwe.	One stayed behind
	Ya sala e se e shwele.	and died.

English

ALPHABET SOUP

Music: Sue Cock Lyrics: Jennifer Tandy

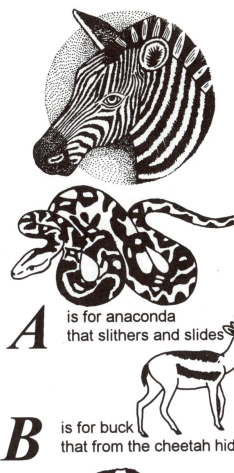

A is for anaconda
that slithers and slides

B is for buck
that from the cheetah hides

C is for chameleon
that is camouflaged
in a flash

D is for dolphin
who dives with a splash

35

E is for eagle
predator in the night

F is for ferret
with a nasty bite

G is for a goat
that leaps over rocky
mountains with ease

H is a horse
that when irritated
kicks off its fleas

I is an iguana
a cold blooded reptile

sli-thers and slides in the night
B is for
F is for
buck that from the chee-tah hides
fer-ret with a nas-ty bite

Y is for yak
that is hairy of course

Z is a zebra
a type of wild horse

A nd that is the end of
my alphabet soup,
alphabet soup!

L is for leopard that creeps and runs free

P is for a porpoise that

has many charms   Q is for quail, a

isiZulu

Kwesukesukel' uGege
Wagay' umcab' uGege
Wavub' amas' uGege
Wabind' ukhez' uGege
Wazishuka wazishuk' uGege
Wazishuka wazishuk' uGege.

There once was a child, Gege.
Gege ground the mielies
Gege mixed the sour milk
Gege choked on the spoon
Gege shook and shook herself.

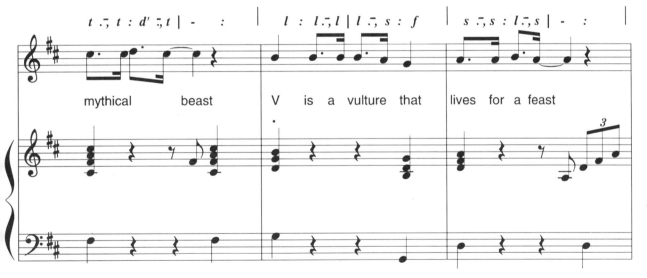

isiZulu

Ngubani lo?
UYeye.
Uhamba nobani?
Nonina.
Umphatheleni?
Amasi.
Ngembiza enjani?
Ebomvu.
Engakanani?
Enkulu.
Awuu, siy' esikolweni.
Awuu, siy' esikolweni.

Who is this?
Yeye.
With whom is she walking?
With her mother.
What is she holding for her?
Sour milk.
In what sort of pot?
A red one.
What size?
A big one.
Oh no, we are going to school!
Oh no, we are going to school!

IMPUKU NEKATI

isiXhosa

Im- pu- ku ne- ka- ti zi- ya- kha- la- kha- la. Im- pu- ku ne- ka- ti zi- ya- kha- la- kha- la. Zi- thi nyau, nyau, zi- thi nyau, nyau, nyau. Zi- thi nyau, nyau, zi- thi nyau, nyau, nyau.

Afrikaans

Trippe trappe trone
Die varkies in die bone
Die koeitjies in die klawer
Die perdjies in die hawer
Wens dat kindjie groter was
om al die diertjies op te pas.

Jick, jack, jeans
Piglets in the beans
Calves in the clover
Ponies in the hay
Wish my child was older
to look after them all day.

Impuku nekati ziyakhalakhala
(Repeat)

Zithi nyau, nyau,
zithi nyau, nyau, nyau.
(Repeat)

The mouse and the cat are crying
They say 'meauw, meauw',
they say 'meauw, meauw, meauw'.

DEMAZANA

isiZulu

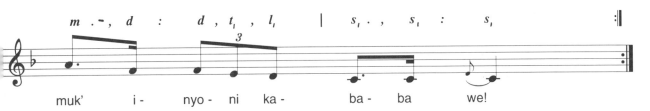

We, Demazana,
Demazana, Demazana
yemuk' inyoni kababa we!
Demazana, Demazana
yemuk' inyoni kababa we!

Hey, Demazana,
Demazana, Demazana,
leave father's bird alone!

isiXhosa

Molo we katshana
Uyaphi we katshana?
Ndiya edolophini
Uyokuthenga ntoni?
Ndiyothenga umnqwazi
Umnqwazi?
Umnqwazi?
Andizange ndilibone
ikat' lithwele umnqwazi!

Hello little cat
Where are you going, little cat?
I am going to town
What are you going to buy?
I am going to go and buy a hat
A hat?
A hat?
I have never seen
a cat wearing a hat!

MAATJIE KLEIN

Afrikaans

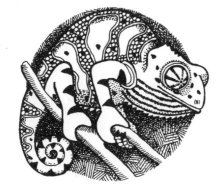

isiZulu

Mina ngiyisicathulo
Mina ngiyisicathulo
Bonke abantu
banyathelwa ngami
Manje sengigugile
Manje sengigugile
Senginje, senginje
Senginjenjenje.

I am a shoe
I am a shoe
All the people
wear me
Now I am old
Now I am old
Now I am like this, like this
Now I am like this.

Maatjie klein kom dans met my
Al twee hande kan jy kry
Links en regs dan 'n draai
In die rondte lekker swaai

Met ons hande klap, klap, klap
Met die voete trap, trap, trap
Links en regs dan 'n draai
In die rondte lekker swaai

Met ons koppe knik, knik, knik
Met die vingers tik, tik, tik
Links en regs dan 'n draai
In die rondte lekker swaai.

Little friend come and dance with me
You may hold both hands
Left and right and then a twirl
In a circle gaily swirl

With our hands we clap, clap, clap
With our feet we stamp, stamp, stamp
Left and right and then a twirl
In a circle gaily swirl

With our heads we nod, nod, nod
With our fingers tap, tap, tap
Left and right and then a twirl
In a circle gaily swirl.

PUNCHINELLO

English

Look who's here,
Punchinello, little fellow
Look who's here,
Punchinello from the zoo

What can you do?
Punchinello, little fellow
What can you do?
Punchinello from the zoo

We can do it too,
Punchinello, little fellow
We can do it too,
Punchinello from the zoo

Who do you choose?
Punchinello, little fellow
Who do you choose?
Punchinello from the zoo.

(Repeat last three verses)

FIELA

seSotho

Fiela, fiela, fiela ngwanana
Fiela ngwanana,
o se jele matlakaleng!
(Repeat)

Mmangwane ke tjobolo
Tjobolo ya mosadi
Feila ngwanana,
o se jele matlakaleng!
(Repeat)

Sweep, sweep, sweep girl
Sweep girl, don't eat
in that dirty place!

Aunt is a fierce person
A fierce woman
Sweep girl, don't eat
in that dirty place!

BABA MNUMZANE
isiZulu

Baba, mnumzane
Uyeye
sivulele singene
(Repeat)

Sangena, sangena,
sangena phakathi.
(Repeat)

Father, sir
Oh yea
open for us so that we can come in

We are entering, we are entering,
we are entering inside.

RA ŠILA MIELIE
sePedi

Ra šila šila mielie mielie
Ngwana wa batho!
(Repeat)

O, darlie wa tsamaya lerato le fedile
Darlie wa tsamaya lerato le fedile.
(Repeat)

We ground and ground the mielies
Poor child!

Oh, darling left, the love was gone
Darling left, the love was gone.

IF THE WORLD

English

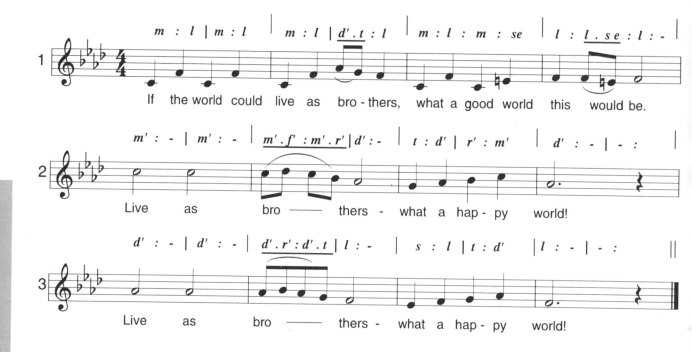

isiZulu

Vuka mfana
Hamb' uy' es'kolweni
Cha, angifuni
Ziph' izinkomo?
Zisempumalanga
Ngubani ozozilanda?
Bathi nguwe mfana
Bathi nguwe mfana.

Wake up young boy
Go to school
No, I don't want to
Where are the cattle?
They are in the east
Who will fetch them?
They say it's you, young boy
They say it's you, young boy.

If the world could live as brothers,
what a good world this would be
Live as brothers -
what a happy world!
Live as brothers -
what a happy world!

UTHANDO LWAKHE
isiZulu

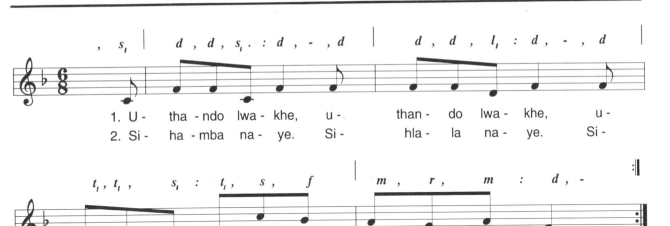

Uthando lwakhe
(Repeat three times)
luyamangalisa

Sihamba naye
Sihlala naye
Silala naye
Sivuka naye.

His love
is amazing

We walk with Him
We live with Him
We sleep with Him
We wake with Him.

I see the moon
and the moon sees me
God bless the moon
and God bless me.

TSHOLLELA

seSotho

Tshollela moya wa hao, Jesu
(Repeat)
Di pelong tsa rona, Jesu
Tshollela moya wa hao, Jesu.

Pour out your spirit, Jesus
In our hearts, Jesus
Pour out your spirit, Jesus.

* Only sung from the second time through

THUMA MINA

isiZulu

Thuma mina
(Repeat three times)
Nkosi yam'

Sengiyavuma
(Repeat three times)
Nkosi yam'

Sengiyabonga
(Repeat three times)
Nkosi yam'

Alleluia
(Repeat three times)
Nkosi yam'

Send me, my God

I agree, my God

I am thankful, my God

Alleluia, my God.

GOD BLESS AFRICA

English

Music: Sue Cock   Prayer: Trevor Huddleston

God bless Africa
(Repeat)
Guard her children,
guide her leaders
and give her peace,
for Jesus Christ's sake, amen.

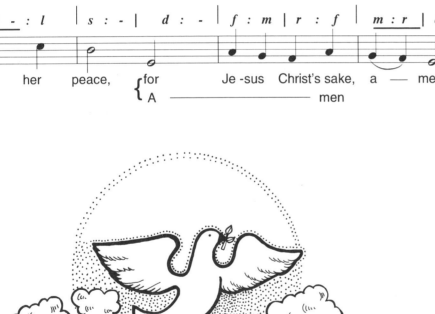

UKUTHULA

isiZulu

Peace, peace
in this world of sin
Alleluia,
the blood of Jesus whispers peace.

redemption
praise
faith
victory
comfort
peace

Zulu words overleaf

Ukuthula, ukuthula
kulo mhlaba wezono
Alleluia,
igazi likaJesu linyenyez' *ukuthula*

Usindiso, usindiso
kulo mhlaba wezono
Alleluia,
igazi likaJesu linyenyez' *usindiso*

Ukubonga, ukubonga
kulo mhlaba wezono
Alleluia,
igazi likaJesu linyenyez' *ukubonga*

Ukukholwa, ukukholwa
kulo mhlaba wezono
Alleleia,
igazi likaJesu linyenyez' *ukukholwa*

Ukunqoba, ukunqoba
kulo mhlaba wezono
Alleluia,
igazi likaJesu linyenyez' *ukunqoba*

Induduzo, induduzo
kulo mhlaba wezono
Alleluia,
igazi likaJesu linyenyez' *induduzo*

Ukuthula, ukuthula
kulo mhlaba wezono
Alleluia,
igazi likaJesu linyenyez' *ukuthula.*

PRONUNCIATION

This pronunciation guide only covers the sounds that **are not similar to English** for the songs and rhymes in this book - it is not a complete table of all pronunciation points for the languages indicated. Examples of words in which the sounds occur are taken from the songs and rhymes. Where no example is given, either the sound does not occur in the language, or it does not appear in the songs and rhymes.

If you need to know how to pronounce a particular sound, check the first column for the written form. Then look across to the second column for an English word that has the same sound (or an explanation of how it is pronounced if the sound does not occur in English). Finally check the example given under the particular language of the song or rhyme.

To ensure accurate pronunciation, it is important to use the cassette tape.

isiZulu, isiXhosa, seSotho, sePedi, seTswana

	Equivalent English sound or explanation	isiZulu	isiXhosa	seSotho	sePedi	seTswana
→a	b*a*sket	ub*a*b*a*	ndiy*a*	h*a*ra	g*a*mang	w*a*
e	*e*gg	bh*e*ka	lithw*e*le	l*e*betse	f*e*dile	*e* nngwe
i	th*i*ef	s*i*hamba	uyaph*i*?	letswa*i*	d*i*kgomo	s*i*la
o	m*o*re	mad*o*da	m*o*lo	mahl*o*	dik*o*mo	n*o*nyane
→u	l*oo*k	v*u*kani	*u*yaphi?	r*u*ri		p*u*la
e*	m*ea*t			r*e*	l*e*rato	r*e*
o*	t*oo*th			*o* jele	bath*o*	f*o*fa
th	*t*ea	ze*th*u	li*th*wele	se*th*unya	rama*th*eka	*th*aro
ph	*p*arty	ama*ph*iko	uya*ph*i?		*ph*irima	a re i*ph*itleng
kh	*k*ick	isi*kh*ova	ziya*kh*ala			
t	as for the English sounds 'p', 't' and 'k'	eMon*t*i	ika*t*i	*t*ama*t*i		
p	but no air comes out of the mouth as	em*p*umalanga	im*p*uku	*p*ere		*p*ula
k	the sound is made.			*k*ama		*k*ana
k	sometimes pronounced as a soft English 'g' sound. in Zulu		e*k*useni			
g	add friction to the 'g' sound - much like the Afrikaans word for insect 'gogo' in sePedi and seTswana				*g*amang	*g*odimo
kg	'k' plus the g described above				di*kg*omo	
r	heavily rolled 'r' sound.			*r*ona	phi*r*ima	tha*r*o
š	*sh*ake					*š*ila

	Equivalent English sound or explanation	isiZulu	isiXhosa	seSotho	sePedi	seTswana
tl	a fast pronunciation of the *tl* in nea*tl*y			*tl*apa	*tl*ala	i phi*tl*eng
ts	ca*ts* - the sound is pronounced sharply			le*ts*wai	le*ts*atsi	fe*ts*a
tsh	as for **ts** but air is released as the sound is made in seSotho, sePedi and seTswana			*tsh*imo		*tsh*aba
tsh	sco*tch* - the sound is pronounced sharply in isiZulu and isiXhosa	ka*tsh*ana	ka*tsh*ana			
tj	as for **tsh** in isiZulu and isiXhosa above			*tj*obolo		
hl	Put the tongue in the position for saying an 'l'. While saying 'lll...' and keeping the tip of the tongue on the palate, blow air out of the sides of the tongue.	zim*hl*ophe		ma*hl*o		
dl	It is pronounced in the same way as **hl** except that it is voiced - hum as the sound is produced.	izan*dl*a				

Clicks

q	Put the tip of the tongue against the roof of the mouth on the ridge behind the top teeth. Put the back of the tongue in the position for saying 'k'. Pull the tongue back sharply to make the click sound.	*q*wa				
qh	As for **q** but release air as the sound is made.	sa*qh*uma				
gq	As for **q** but hum as you say the sound - don't say the 'g'.	isi*gq*oko				
nq	As for **q** but with an 'n' before the click sound.	i*nq*e	um*nq*wazi			
c	Put the tip of the tongue just behind the top teeth. Put the back of the tongue in the position for saying 'k'. Pull the tip of the tongue away sharply.	u*c*ikicane				
ch	As for **c** but release air as the sound is made.	*ch*a				

* SeSotho, SePedi and seTswana have seven vowels. There are two values for **o** and **e** which are not differentiated in the written form. The cassette tape will help with the pronunciation.

	Equivalent English sound or explanation	**Afrikaans**
e	S*a*rah	sê
oo	Pronounced as two syllables *koo-erp*	k*oo*p
ou	gr*ow* - when it occurs at the end of a word	g*ou*
ei	l*ay*er	*ei*ers
v	*f*at - when it occurs at the beginning of a word	*v*ol
w	*v*ery - when it occurs at the beginning of a word	*w*ol
	*w*itch - elsewhere	s*w*aai
r	rolled but may fall away at the end of a word	t*r*ein
g	add friction to the 'g' sound - sounded like an 'h' at the back of the throat	ma*g*ie
djie	hard 'k' as in han*ky*	kin*djie*
tjie	hard 'k' as in han*ky*	voe*tjie*
ng	in the middle of a word - 'nya' as in *n*ew	aa*ng*ekruip